The Bush Theatre and Recorded Delivery present

by Alecky Blythe
7 June – 1 July 2006

Cast

(in alphabetical order)

Roy/Bernard/Peter/Jack	**Jason Barnett**
Roberta/Pat	**Alecky Blythe**
Geoff/Dudley	**Ian Dunn**
Maureen	**Miranda Hart**
Margaret/Liz	**Claire Lichie**

Director	**Matthew Dunster**
Designer	**Anna Bliss Scully**
Lighting Designer	**David Holmes**
Movement Director	**Georgina Lamb**
Producer for Recorded Delivery	**James Allenby**

Press Representation	**Alexandra Gammie** **020 7837 8333**

Graphic Design	**Stem Design** **www.stemdesign.co.uk**

Some places and names have been changed.

Cruising was initially developed at The Actors Centre and then commissioned by The Bush Theatre.

Recorded Delivery is grateful for the support of a project grant from Arts Council, England. The Bush Theatre gratefully acknowledges the support of The Mercers' Company and Nick Hern Books.

Jason Barnett Roy/Bernard/Peter/Jack

Theatre includes Alf Ramsey in *The 1966 World Cup* (National tour/BAC), *Jason and the Argonauts, Party Time* and *One For The Road* (BAC), *All The Right People Come Here* (Tristan Bates Theatre/Wimbledon Studio), *Come Out Eli* (Cork Festival), *Someone Who'll Watch Over Me* (National Theatre Studio), *A Man For All Seasons* (Young Vic Studio), *Burn* and *Julius Caesar* (Synergy Theatre Project/Prison's tour), *Merlin* (Riverside Studios), *Dealer's Choice* (Orange Tree Theatre), *The Day of All Days – Flight 5065* (London Eye/Lift Africa '05), *John Dryden's Tempest* and *The Battle of Alcazar* (Shakespeare's Globe, Education) and *Amato Saltone* (National Theatre/Shunt Vaults).

Television credits include *The Bill, The Sight, Dreamteam, Fur TV, Bulla, Uncut Funk, Little Britain,* and the current series' of *Dead Ringers* and *Stupid!*

Film credits include *One Man and His Dog, Plotless* and *The Refugee* (Notting Hill Film Festival Winner).

Jason is a BBC Radio Drama 'Norman Beaton Fellowship' finalist.

Ian Dunn Geoff/Dudley

Theatre includes *Osama the Hero* and *A Single Act* (Hampstead Theatre), *Project C: On Principle* (BAC), *A Doll's House* (Southwark Playhouse), *Terrorism, Fucking Games, Toast, I Am Yours* and *Babies* (Royal Court), *Luminosity, Love Play* (RSC), *Chips With Everything* and *Somewhere* (National Theatre), *Our Boys* (Donmar Warehouse/Derby Playhouse), *Six Degrees of Separation* (Royal Court/Comedy Theatre), *A Prayer For Wings* (tour), *Hidden Laughter* (Vaudeville), *Forget Me Not Lane* (Greenwich), *Invisible Friends, Wolf at the Door* and *Brighton Beach* (Scarborough).

Television includes *Eastenders, Holby City, Doctors, Murphy's Law, Sea of Souls, Red Cap, Girls in Love, Trust, London's Burning, Peak Practice, Bad Girls, The Bill, Reach for the Moon, Bliss, Stone, Scissors & Paper, Gulliver's Travels, Shine on Harvey Moon, Casualty, Desmonds, Jackanory: The Gulf, The Merrihill Millionaires, A Touch of Frost, Soldier Soldier, Children of the North* and *Sweet Capital Lives*.

Film includes *American Friends* and *Bye Bye Baby*.

Miranda Hart Maureen

Miranda Hart is a comedy writer and actress.

Her television credits include *Jack Dee's Leud Balloon, Hyperdrive, Nighty Night, My Family and Other Animals, Absolutely Fabulous, The Vicar of Dibley, French and Saunders* and *Smack the Pony*.

Radio includes *Giles Wembley Hogg Goes Off, The 99p Challenge* and *At Home With Snails* (all for BBC Radio 4).

As a writer and stand-up Miranda has written and performed a number of critically acclaimed solo shows at the Edinburgh Festival and in London including *Miranda Hart's House Party* (Pleasance Theatre, Edinburgh), *It's All About Me* (Soho Theatre) and *Miranda Hart-Throbs!* (Pleasance Theatre, Edinburgh). She regularly performs on the comedy circuit. Further writing credits include a sitcom in development with the BBC, *Miranda Hart's Joke Shop* and *Smack the Pony* for Channel 4.

Miranda was also in Recorded Delivery's Time Out Award Winning *Come Out Eli* at the Arcola and BAC. She studied acting at ALRA.

Claire Lichie Margaret/Liz

Claire trained at the Guildford School of Acting.

Theatre includes *Gladiator Games* (Sheffield Crucible & Theatre Royal, Stratford East), *Way To Heaven* (Royal Court Theatre), Recorded Delivery productions: *Cruising* and *All The Right People Come Here* (Rough Cut at The Bush Theatre), *Miss Private View* (Soho Theatre), *Lovers* (Gielgud Theatre), *Given A Way* (Soho Theatre), *The Witch of Edmonton* (Southwark Playhouse), *Blue Funk* (Old Red Lion Theatre), *Love's Labour's Lost* (Etcetera Theatre), *The Snow Queen* (National Tour) and *Yerma* (Southwark Playhouse).

Film includes *Inbetweeners* (Universal Pictures).

TV includes *Agony*.

Alecky Blythe Writer *and* Roberta/Pat

Alecky Blythe trained at Mountview Theatre School. She is the Founder and Artistic Director of Recorded Delivery whose first production *Come Out Eli* at the Arcola (Time Out Award for Best Production On The Fringe) transferred to BAC (Critics Choice Season). Her subsequent Recorded Delivery productions include *All the Right People Come Here* (New Wimbledon Theatre), *The Day of All The Days* (Café Direct London Eye Festival) and *I only Came Here For Six Months* (British Council. KVS and Les Halles, Brussels). Recorded Delivery is a resident company at the Actors Centre.

Alecky's verbatim work with other companies includes *Strawberry Fields* (Pentabus, National tour), *A Man in a Box* (National Theatre Studio) and as a collaborator with Talking Birds for The Dark Room 2006 (The John Osborne Arvon Centre). She is currently under commission at The Royal Court, researching a project with The National Theatre's Education Department and co-producing the screen adaptation of *Come Out Eli* with Channel 4.

Matthew Dunster Director

Matthew is an Associate Director of The Young Vic and a founder member of The Work Theatre Collective.

Directing work includes *Project B* (The Work), *Some Voices* (Young Vic), *Port Authority* (Liverpool Everyman) and *Project D: I'm Mediocre* (The Work).

Writing includes *You Used To* (Contact), *Tell Me* (Contact and Donmar Warehouse) and *Two Clouds Over Eden* (Royal Exchange).

As an actor, recent theatre credits include *Toast, Plasticine, Under The Whaleback, Harvest* (Royal Court), *The Daughter-in-Law* (Young Vic), *The Permanent Way* (RNT/Out of Joint), *Project C: On Principle* (The Work) and *Fallen Angels* (Fecund Theatre).

Televison includes *Murder Prevention, Conviction, No Angels, Coronation Street, Gimme Gimme Gimme, True Voice of Rape, Vincent, Silent Witness, Heartbeat, Always And Everyone, Golden Collar, Into the Fire, Walking On The Moon, Doctors, Casualty, Spring Hill* and *Peter Kay's Driven To Distraction*.

Film includes *Peaches* and *Hello You*.

Anna Bliss Scully Designer

Anna trained at Wimbledon School of Art and with the National Youth Theatre of Wales.

Her designs include *Showstopper* (Theatre Royal, Bury St. Edmunds), *Splendour* (Cohden Club), *The Merchant of Venice* (Orange Tree Theatre), *Amy Evans' Strike* (Courtyard@Covent Garden), *A Midsummer Night's Dream* (Young Vic Love Shorts), *The Morals of Modern Day Myths* (Sherman Theatre Cardiff), *The Soldier* (Edinburgh/RADA), *However Do You Want Me?* (Hen & Chickens), *Buzz* (Sgript Cymru), *Jacob Jacobson* (Bloomsbury Theatre), *Monster* for Escape Artists (Royal Opera House/Tour).

She is Joint Artistic Director of True/Fiction Theatre, for whom she has also designed *Will Eno Shorts*, *Friction*, *Bash: Latterday Plays* and *Riddance*.

Work as an Assistant Designer includes *Baba Yaga* (Mervyn Millar/BAC), *The Marriage of Figaro* and *Orpheus In The Underworld* (both British Youth Opera).

David Holmes Lighting Designer

David trained at the Theatre Royal, Glasgow and the Guildhall School of Music and Drama.

Theatre credits include Monteverdi's *Harvey* (Manchester Royal Exchange), *Stallerhof* (Southwark Playhouse), *The Factory Girls* and *Lysistrata* (Arcola Theatre), *Fijis* for Dance Umbrella at the South Bank Centre and The Place, London, *The Leningrad Siege* (Wilton's Music Hall, London), *The Trestle at Pope Lick Creek* (Studio, Manchester Royal Exchange and Southwark Playhouse), *L'Orfeo* (Greenwich), *Woman In Mind* and *Be My Baby* (Salisbury), *Car Thieves* (Birmingham), *The Fantasticks*, *Ain't Misbehavin'*, *House* and *Garden* and *Cleo, Camping, Emmanuelle and Dick* (Harrogate), *The Secret Rapture* (Chichester), *Twelfth Night* (Cambridge), *Look Back In Anger* and *The Mentalists* (Exeter), *The Water Engine*, *Photos of Religion* and *A State of Innocence* (Theatre 503, Battersea), *Cosi fan Tutte* (Guildhall School), *The Tempest* and *The Sleeper's Den* (Southwark).

Future projects include *Cyrano de Bergerac* at Manchester Royal Exchange, *The Beggar's Opera* and *The Threepenny Opera* for Trinity College of Music and *Tomorrow Morning* (New End Theatre, Hampstead).

David was also Associate to lighting designers Hugh Vanstone and Howard Harrison for seven years.

Georgina Lamb Movement Director

Georgina is creative associate of Frantic Assembly and works extensively with the company as a collaborator and performer.

Other directing credits include Lyric Hammersmith, Jackson's Lane, Battersea Arts Centre, Pleasance Edinburgh, National Youth Theatre, OnO Theatre Co, West Sussex Youth Theatre, The Baltic, Newcastle and Bigfoot/London Talent.

As a movement director/choreographer credits include Oxford Stage Company, Oily Carte, Jet Theatre Co, Half Moon young people's theatre, Manchester Met School of Theatre, The Cresset Peterborough and The Work Collective.

Performing credits include Royal National Theatre, National Theatre of Scotland, Frantic Assembly, Stephen Joseph Theatre Scarborough, Trestle Theatre Co, Leicester Haymarket, Lyric Hammersmith, Royal Opera House, Library Manchester, Pilot Theatre Co, Fecund Theatre, Gecko and RNT Studio.

The Bush Theatre Co-Producer

The Bush Theatre opened in April 1972 in the upstairs dining room of The Bush Hotel, Shepherds Bush Green. The room had previously served as Lionel Blair's dance studio. Since then, The Bush has become one of the country's leading new writing venues with over 350 productions, premiering the finest new writing talent.

Playwrights whose works have been performed at The Bush include: Stephen Poliakoff, Robert Holman, Tina Brown, Snoo Wilson, John Byrne, Ron Hutchinson, Terry Johnson, Beth Henley, Kevin Elyot, Doug Lucie, Dusty Hughes, Sharman Macdonald, Billy Roche, Tony Kushner, Catherine Johnson, Philip Ridley, Richard Cameron, Jonathan Harvey, Richard Zajdlic, Naomi Wallace, David Eldridge, Conor McPherson, Joe Penhall, Helen Blakeman, Lucy Gannon, Mark O'Rowe and Charlotte Jones.

The theatre has also attracted major acting and directing talents including Bob Hoskins, Alan Rickman, Antony Sher, Stephen Rea, Frances Barber, Lindsay Duncan, Brian Cox, Kate Beckinsale, Patricia Hodge, Simon Callow, Alison Steadman, Jim Broadbent, Tim Roth, Jane Horrocks, Gwen Taylor, Mike Leigh, Mike Figgis, Mike Newell and Richard Wilson. Victoria Wood and Julie Walters first worked together at The Bush, and Victoria wrote her first sketch on an old typewriter she found backstage.

In over 30 years, The Bush has won over one hundred awards and recently received The Peggy Ramsay Foundation Project Award. Bush plays, including most recently *The Glee Club*, have transferred to the West End. Off-Broadway transfers include *Howie the Rookie* and *Resident Alien*. Film adaptations include *Beautiful Thing* and *Disco Pigs*. Bush productions have toured throughout Britain, Europe, North America and Asia, most recently *Stitching*, *adrenalin... heart* (representing the UK in the Tokyo International Arts Festival, 2004) *The Glee Club* (2004), *After The End* (UK, Europe and New York, 2006) and a national number one tour of *Mammals* (2006).

Every year The Bush receives over fifteen hundred scripts through the post, and every one is read. This is one small part of a comprehensive Writers' Development Programme, which includes commissions, bursaries, one-to-one dramaturgy, masterclasses, workshops and readings.

According to The Sunday Times:

"What happens at The Bush today is at the very heart of tomorrow's theatre"

That's why we read all the scripts and will continue to do so.

Mike Bradwell　　**Fiona Clark**
Artistic Director　　Executive Producer

At The Bush Theatre

Artistic Director	**Mike Bradwell**
Executive Producer	**Fiona Clark**
Finance Manager	**Dave Smith**
Literary Manager	**Abigail Gonda**
Marketing Manager	**Nicki Marsh**
Production Manager	**Robert Holmes**
Theatre Administrator	**Nic Wass**
Resident Stage Manager	**Ros Terry**
Chief Technician	**Sam Shortt**
Literary Assistant	**Raphael Martin**
Administrative Assistant	**Lydia Fraser-Ward**
Box Office Supervisor	**Darren Elliott**
Box Office Assistants	**Gail MacLeod** **Margaret-Ann Bain**
Front of House Duty Managers	**Kellie Batchelor** **Adrian Christopher** **Siobhan King-Spooner** **Catherine Nix-Collins** **Lois Tucker**
Duty Technicians	**Helen Spall** **Tom White**
Associate Artists	**Tanya Burns** **Es Devlin** **Richard Jordan** **Paul Miller**
Pearson Playwright in Residence	**Jack Thorne**

The Bush Theatre
Shepherds Bush Green
London W12 8QD

Box Office: 020 7610 4224
www.bushtheatre.co.uk

Be There At The Beginning

The Bush Theatre is a writer's theatre – dedicated to commissioning, developing and producing exclusively new plays. Up to seven writers each year are commissioned and we offer a bespoke programme of workshops and one-to-one dramaturgy to develop their plays. Our international reputation of over thirty years is built on consistently producing the very best work to the very highest standard.

With your help this work can continue to flourish.

The Bush Theatre's Patron Scheme delivers an exciting range of opportunities for individual and corporate giving, offering a closer relationship with the theatre and a wide range of benefits from ticket offers to special events. Above all, it is an ideal way to acknowledge your support for one of the world's greatest new writing theatres.

To join, please pick up an information pack from the foyer, call 020 7602 3703 or email info@bushtheatre.co.uk

We would like to thank our current members and invite you to join them!

Rookies
Anonymous
Ross Anderson
Geraldine Caufield
Nina Drucker
John Gowers
Ms Sian Hansen
Lucy Heller
Mr G Hopkinson
Joyce Hytner, ACT IV
Casarotto Ramsay &
 Associates Ltd
Robin Kermode
Ray Miles
Mr & Mrs Malcolm Ogden
John & Jacqui Pearson
 Radfin
Clare Rich and Robert
 Marshall
Mark Roberts
Tracey Scoffield
Martin Shenfield
Alison Winter

Beautiful Things
Anonymous
Alan Brodie
Kate Brooke
David Brooks
Clive Butler
Matthew Byam Shaw
Jeremy Conway
Clyde Cooper
Mike Figgis
Vivien Goodwin
Sheila Hancock
David Hare
Laurie Marsh
Michael McCoy
Mr & Mrs A Radcliffe
John Reynolds
Barry Serjent
John & Tita Shakeshaft
Brian D Smith
Barrie & Roxanne Wilson

Glee Club
Anonymous
Jim Broadbent
Curtis Brown Group Ltd
Alan Rickman

Handful of Stars
Gianni Alen-Buckley

Lone Star
Princess of Darkness

Bronze Corporate Membership
Anonymous
Act Productions Ltd

Silver Corporate Membership
Anonymous
The Agency (London) Ltd

Platinum Corporate Membership
Anonymous

Recorded Delivery Co-Producer

Recorded Delivery was founded by Alecky Blythe in 2003, after she learnt an innovative verbatim technique to create plays from Mark Wing-Davey at the Actors Centre. The company was subsequently offered the space to create their first show *Come Out Eli*, which was presented as a work in progress at the Tristan Bates Theatre, where it secured a run at the Arcola. After its success, winning the Time Out Award 2004 for The Best Production on the Fringe and transferring to BAC for the Critics' Choice Season, Recorded Delivery have become a resident company at the Actors Centre, where they continue to receive invaluable support and Arts Council funding to develop new work. They created two shows under this residency, *All the Right People Come Here* (New Wimbledon Studio, June 2005) and the first draft of *Cruising* (Tristan Bates Theatre, February 2005). *Come Out Eli*, after its success at The Arcola and later at The BAC, is being co-produced as a film of the same name with Channel 4.

'This is astonishing documentary theatre...
at times breathtaking... Absolutely riveting'

Daily Telegraph on *Come Out Eli*

Recorded Delivery is grateful for the support of Arts Council, England and The Actors Centre.
www.recordeddelivery.net

CRUISING

Alecky Blythe

Introduction

by Alecky Blythe

Verbatim theatre first attracted me when I was looking at alternative ways of creating work for myself as an actress. An inspiring workshop, 'Drama without Paper', run by Mark Wing-Davey at the Actors Centre, triggered the necessary creative spark that has been burning healthily ever since. Mark taught a technique that he had acquired and adapted from Anna Deavere Smith with whom he had worked in New York. The verbatim technique requires no transcribing but works directly from the interview via earphones. The exact speech pattern of the interviewee – including coughs, stutters and non sequiturs – is faithfully reproduced. The difference Mark introduced was to perform the interviews still wearing the earphones. This stopped the actors from ever falling into their own speech patterns, and the performances were all the more compelling for it. Anna had only used the earphones in rehearsals.

The Actors Centre, where Recorded Delivery is now a resident company, supported an idea for a verbatim play and helped set up the company, offering rehearsal and performance space to try something out. With Mark as my mentor, I created *Come Out Eli*. The idea for the play itself was to interview people about their fears, so an armed siege in nearby Hackney Central, where crowds had gathered to watch the 'spectacle', seemed the ideal place to collect interviews. As the stand-off between the police and Eli the gunman continued into its third week, the curiosity and, in some cases, outrage of the locals grew, and I simply gathered their personal stories about how they had been affected. I was drawn to the fantastically diverse range of people who for once had a common talking point. The topic of fear had been the starting point for the play which then grew into something quite different. Not only did the siege give the piece a narrative structure but the dramatic setting of the stand-off was ideal for uninhibited speech because the interviewees were more engaged in what was going on (or not) than the pressure of an interview situation.

In subsequent pieces I have tried to find a setting which takes the interviewee's attention off the microphone as much as possible. Most verbatim theatre is created from interviews that have obviously been set up, leading to a certain self-consciousness in the characters. This approach can be very illuminating, but I am aiming for a more 'fly on the wall' documentary style as this can lead to more dramatic situations. *Cruising* shifts between monologues with Maureen, the protagonist through whom the narrative weaves, and scenes with her friends that illustrate and push the narrative on. Also, by meeting her in public and private, a more rounded character is created. However, when I first interviewed her, I was so intrigued by her that my original idea was to make a one-woman show. After *Eli*, which had forty-seven characters, *All The Right People Come Here* and *Strawberry Fields,* both with too many characters to count, a show focusing on one or a few characters was an exciting new challenge.

Maureen was a woman I interviewed for *Strawberry Fields,* which was about the effects of modern farming methods on the land and the community in the rural idyll of Herefordshire where she lives. In *Strawberry Fields* she immediately came across as a very interesting and likeable character: all the actors wanted to play her. She had the potential to command more than just a walk-on part, so I ventured to interview her again to see what else she had to reveal. Two-and-a-half hours later, the tape was still running, and the idea for *Cruising* had been conceived. What made her story extraordinary – apart from her healthy libido – was an attitude towards men and love which mirrored the views of women fifty years younger. She spoke about her broken heart as if she were a love-struck teenager not a worldly widow of seventy-two with two married children. Her story threw up so many questions. How much do we mature emotion-ally? Do we not learn from our mistakes? Are one-night stands still as possible and, if so, as painful in one's seventies as in one's twenties? A whole new world of pensioners in search of passion had been discovered through Maureen, and she was willing to take me on her journey to explore it.

In the early stages of research, as well as talking to her contacts – i.e. friends in a similar situation and past failed dates – other pensioners were interviewed. However, when Maureen's friend Margaret announced her engagement to Geoff, that story became the main narrative thrust of the piece as it fuelled Maureen's own feelings of loneliness and the need to find love. The natural course of events had produced their own dramatic situation. The love story had not happened for Maureen as she had hoped, but for her good friend Margaret. Maureen is left at the end of the play still broken-hearted, consoling herself with her busy life and having resorted to buying a cat for company. This particular moment in time catches her in an unusually melancholy mood, not her typical persona but one which maybe only her cat gets to see. Since then, she has inevitably bounced back and is knocking off e-mails to men from all over the UK with renewed vigour. Although this is undoubtedly how she would like to be remembered, it would not make for such a poignant ending.

I did not set out to make a biographical documentary, but a piece of drama which has been edited and therefore warped in some way for dramatic purposes. There is, of course, a moral responsibility to consider when dealing with and presenting real life, one which I endeavour to uphold. Nonetheless, the end result is a play created from real life that has been processed firstly by the editing of the material and secondly by the performance. No matter how truthful the methods of representation, the characters inevitably take on a life of their own once nurtured by the director and presented by the actors. However, all the while the audience know that these are the words of real people, and this is the magic of the technique.

Special thanks to Maureen, Margaret and Geoff and all those who contributed their stories.

6

Characters (*in order of appearance*)

FATHER TOWNSEND, *mid-thirties. He has a beard*
MAUREEN, *early seventies. She wears a hearing aid and colourful jewellery with her outfit. Reading glasses hang on a chain around her neck*
PAT, *early forties. Trousers and a beige blouse*
LIZ, *mid-forties. Long denim skirt and sequined pumps*
JOHN, *eighty. Blazer and a tie*
ROY, *late sixties. Checked shirt and corduroy trousers*
ROBERTA, *sixty. Sleeveless puffa jacket and a skirt*
BERNARD, *seventy-eight. Black shirt and a bright red jumper*
DUDLEY, *late seventies. White shirt and a black tie*
PETER, *sixty-eight. Dark green fleece and glasses*
MARGARET, *seventy-six. Frilly lilac blouse and a neat little skirt*
GEOFF, *eighty. Blazer with cufflinks and a tie. Metal framed glasses*
JOY, *late sixties. Royal-blue, wide-brimmed hat and matching jacket*
DEREK, *early seventies. Navy suit. Club tie. Glasses*
PAT, *mid-sixties. Lemon-yellow, low-backed dress and feathered hat*
PHOTOGRAPHER, *mid-forties. Black suit*
VIVIAN, *early forties. Floral dress*
JACK, *eighty-two. Grey suit. Pale green shirt and off-white tie with a tie pin. Metal-framed glasses*
WAITRESS, *forties. White shirt and black skirt*

Some names and places have been changed.

Forward slashes (/) indicate the moment when one character is interrupted by another. The dialogue which interrupts is also preceded by a forward slash. Where multiple slashes appear within one speech, the character continues talking with the overlapping dialogue given after the end of their speech. When two characters' adjacent lines begin with a forward slash this indicates they speak simultaneously.

1.

Welcome (2'32")

The Priory Church, Leominster.

A very hot day in June. The organ plays an excerpt from Samson *by Handel as* MARGARET *enters. The congregation whispers and fidgets as they wait for the service to start.*

FATHER TOWNSEND. May the grace of our Lord Jesus Christ, the Love of God, and the fellowship of the Holy Spirit be with you.

CONGREGATION. And also with you.

FATHER. Lovely to be able to welcome you all here, on this beautiful day for a – wonderful occasion. Special welcome, of course, to Margaret and Geoff –

A baby in the congregation begins to fret.

It's uh – a great privilege and pleasure to be conducting this *important* ceremony – and very special cem . . . ceremony. Special welcome to your families, and to all friends, and to all members of this congregation – the choir, and everyone who's come to be with you on this special day. Just a couple of notices before I say the first prayer – erm, in fact only one notice:

The church door slams.

The dreaded subject of confetti –

Soft laughter in the congregation.

– of course you can throw it.

General laughter.

Make a mess. That's great. Okay, let us pray.

God of wonder, and of joy. Send your Holy Spirit and pour into our hearts that most excellent gift of love. That we may worship you now with thankful hearts, and serve you *always* with willing minds. Through Jesus Christ, our Lord, Amen.

CONGREGATION. Amen.

FATHER. First of all, I am required to ask *anyone* present who knows a reason why these persons may not lawfully marry – to declare it.

Silence.

2.

World Cruise (2'46")

MAUREEN*'s living room, comfortable with floral cushioned chairs.*

MAUREEN. When I lost my husband, you know, I was sad – but at the same time I thought, well, I'm sixty-six, and you know, maybe I've got another twenty years, and I must find somebody else. So, um, through an advertisement I put in a magazine – I put in, I put in um, *Yours* magazine, do you know it? I met this gentleman. This wealthy Scotsman – the millionaire – and took me round the world and then he had a prostate operation, and dropped me. (*Laughs.*) We were together two-and-a-half years on and off – and the first year he took me to Bali, for a two – well, he asked me to go for three months – to the Sheraton Hotel in – *Nusa Dua*, but I could only go for two months, cos I had other arrangements. And of course everybody in Leominster thought it was – absolutely unbelievable that I was going out to spend two months in Bali with a man I'd only just met.

He took me to this beautiful place, and a lovely room, you know, and he said, 'That's your part of the wardrobe' an, and he said and he *had* said in the letter he wouldn't expect me to, um, well – he didn't put it like that, but he didn't expect me to have – sex with him straightaway, cos he said, 'You'll be tired.' But actually (*Laughs.*) I wasn't tired at all, and uh, I wanted to change anyway – so I took all m'clothes off and said, 'You might as well see me now.' (*Laughs loudly.*) He was – knocked for six. (*Laughs loudly.*) And so we, um, we consummated our love that night. You see, when you're young you don't think that this can happen when you're at *my* age, you know, just like a real romance – we were making love about three times a day. And I told my doctor and she said it's most unusual for people in our age. Yeah, I mean, he w – he would have been seventy-one then.

When I ring him up he won't talk to me – he puts the phone down. I know, it's very sad. And all my friends say, 'Oh, you're better off without him, it's terrible the way he treated you,' because when we were with my friends, they said I was always so quiet – not – I'm normally not quiet. But they said when I was with him, because he dominated me, and they said he put me down at times. You know. It shows you what men can be like. Yeah. But I was willing to put up with it, you see, I was willing to put up with the bad times for the good times.

Why couldn't he – give me an explanation? Why – he just went away like that? But I've just put it down to the fact he had that operation. I – wrote and asked his brother, but his brother didn't reply. So – from that day to this, I don't know.

3.

Attractive Partners (2'23")

A dating agency near Leamington Spa.

Phones ringing.

PAT. Good afternoon, Attractive Partners, can I help you?

Pause.

No, it's Pat.

Pause.

Oh hi, how are you?

Pause.

I'm all right, thank you, had a bit of a cough and a cold,
but, you know, it's gone now. Doesn't stop me talking.
(*Laughs politely.*)

LIZ. Oh, shame. (*Laughs.*)

PAT. 'Shame,' says my boss.

PAT *continues to speak on the phone in the background as
LIZ speaks. LIZ refers to a file of clients' profiles.*

LIZ. We're called Attractive Partners cos we *want* – people like
this. See? He's seventy-one. So – generally speaking the
people *are* attractive. Some, you know, in a rather – 'sweet'
way, (*Laughs.*) and others in a very macho way.

So you notice that, actually, there are *more* – in the older
age group. Yeah. Look at this lady, for example, she's –
seventy-three. Well, actually she's seventy-four now – look
at her. Without even *interviewing* her, without even
interviewing her –

The phone rings in the background.

– if she sent me that photograph, I would know – that she's
still interested in – in sex. Because she's – made herself
look gorgeous. Unlike – s . . . sweet lady – but, unlike *this*
lady. Who I would say, probably prefers – just playing with
her grandchildren. You know. She will be – she will
definitely be *not* looking for sex, nor her – she's quite
interested, in sex. She's definitely interested. (*Laughing.*)
You can tell, can't you?

Our oldest man – (*Laughing.*) and this is so sweet – he was
– ei . . . eighty-seven when he phoned, to to ex – to ask
about the agency, (PAT *laughing.*) but he lied about his age.
He's actually ninety. But he's *so* lovely – see if I can find /
him –

PAT. / We've matched him, Liz.

LIZ. I know! Ooh, ooh. Let me find the group. Here he is. And
he's lovely. You know, you wouldn't think he was ninety,
would you? Doesn't he look lovely? And, he was rea – and
he's lovely, he's a really good laugh, and everything.

Interesting man, actually. Very gentle man with a sense of humour. Um, I won't – obviously – tell you too much, because . . . We've matched him – oh, she's lovely. Yeah. But you see, we haven't heard back from them yet. When we asked him for some words to describe himself, he said he was alive. (*Laughs.*)

4.

Thirty-Three Men Since (0'14")

MAUREEN's *living room.*

MAUREEN. I've met thirty-three men since then, and I haven't really wanted any of them. (*Laughs.*) But then, of course none of them were millionaires. I don't think any other man'll ever win my heart, you see.

5.

Record (0'29")

A pub in Shrewsbury during a busy lunchtime. MAUREEN *is holding a MiniDisc player and a microphone*

MAUREEN. Record. Right. Say 'Hello'.

JOHN. Little place – well, 'Hello'.

MAUREEN *laughs.*

WAITRESS. Hello. Are you with any of the parties? / No.

MAUREEN. / No.

JOHN. / No no no no, we're just / two.

WAITRESS. / Here we are, so sit here.

MAUREEN. Oh right.

JOHN. Will that do for you? / Well, what do you want to eat? Are we having food?

WAITRESS. / That do for you?

MAUREEN. / You. Yes, I thought – I thought we had booked in the restaurant.

JOHN. Well, I – I said 'Table for two', but um – nobody seems to be aware of it, / so . . .

WAITRESS. / Oh 'ad you?

MAUREEN. / Oh right, that's fine – then, thank you. Well, this is all recording / so um . . .

JOHN. / Yes. Is it? I'll be very good.

MAUREEN *laughs.*

6.

Sleazy (0'53")

Pub, as before.

ROY. No, I mean the Attractive Partners thing is, a fairly, / fairly exclusive – uh, a nice gentle sort of organisation.

ROBERTA. / It's sort of. It doesn't. And it does say that. And you don't feel that / it's sort of – um.

ROY. / Not at all sleazy.

ROBERTA. It's not like – speed dating. We felt it was more – mature.

ROY. They sell themselves very well.

ROBERTA. They do.

ROY. And Liz sold herself very well.

Pause.

ROBERTA. Roy fancied her. He asked her for a date / 'Would you like to . . . '

ROY. / I didn't. I mean, I think Bobby put it that we'd been introduced by a mutual acquaintance.

ROBERTA. That's what we've told people. Yes.

ROY. We haven't told anybody that we'd met / – you know, in the way that we did.

ROBERTA. / No.

ROY. / Well – there's just something, about it which, uh, bit . . .

ROBERTA. / Well –

ROY. . . . slea . . . not sleazy, is it?

ROBERTA. A bit erm – desperate. (*Laughs.*)

7.

Understaffed (0'37")

Pub, as before.

MAUREEN. Actually I saw – I saw you. Over there, about quarter to twelve.

JOHN. I came early / because I – I didn't know what the traffic would / be like, and the – like that.

MAUREEN. / Yes. / Right. Yes yes.

JOHN. But I – I came to have a wander round. I didn't get the . . . Came in here, about quarter past / . . . twelve, something like that.

MAUREEN. / Right, yeah. I – I have eaten in here before. And the last time it was at Christmas, and it was absolutely disgusting / – not the food. /

JOHN. / Oh. / Because

MAUREEN. But they were under / staffed, and . . . Stuff all over the place.

JOHN. / . . . staffed. Well, that's the problem these days. Actually, Thursday's not a bad day – Friday and Saturday, I think there'd be problems.

MAUREEN. / Yes. Um.

JOHN. Yes. Light lunch.

8.

Engaged (1'01")

Pub, as before.

ROY. We met for the first time – not quite halfway – between where I live and where Bobby lives. And I'd been there for an hour, of course, *military* training. Sizing up the place: which would be the best table for me to sit at – and, um. So I was there, and *spot on* time, weren't you?

ROBERTA. Oh yes, I just looked around.

ROY. The door opened, and in she walked. And we laughed immediately, / didn't we?

ROBERTA. / Yes. I just saw him / there –

ROY. / Because it was funny. It was teenage stuff, really, it was *Blind Date*. You know, Cilla Black and that sort thing . . . Well, it – it took off from there, really. Um. That was a year ago. We're engaged, yes.

ROBERTA (*laughs*). Yes.

ROY. Show 'em your –

ROBERTA *shows the ring on her right hand.*

ROBERTA. Well, it's a sort of engagement come Christmas and birthday present, you see. So it's –

ROY. What's it doing on that – ?!

ROBERTA. Well, sometimes I wear it on that finger, sometimes I wear it on that finger, depending on my mood.

Pause.

ROY. Yes, we are engaged to be married.

9.

Cheers (0'35")

Pub, as before.

MAUREEN (*studying the menu*). Rr, rr, rr, rr, rr, rr.

JOHN. What have you had that you've enjoyed, / eating here?

MAUREEN. Well, I've had all of these, I think, because I do come here quite a bit.

JOHN. Aha.

MAUREEN. I think, you know, they're all a fine, erm . . . Oh, I know, I'll go for the – coronation chicken. Cheers anyway. / Cheers.

JOHN. / Yes, cheers. *Iech – Iechyd da.* / And – and *Slainte Mhath*, I think, I – how to say that. Cos my lot hunt, high loch from Caithness – / Have a different greeting, if you're Celtic breeding.

MAUREEN. / Right.

MAUREEN. / *Bonne santé.* Right, yeah.

Time is never wasted when you meet someone, because you always learn something.

10.

Perfect Pauline (1'19")

ROY*'s garden.*

ROBERTA *is throwing a squeezy toy for* ROY*'s dog.*

ROBERTA. When I first arrived, there were – pictures of – 'Perfect Pauline' in every single room, including the bedroom. Even the loo – you couldn't even have a wee-wee without 'Perfect Pauline' staring at you when you were pulling your knickers down. (*Laughs softly.*) Anyway, I've removed most of those. There are a few around, that's fair enough I think. The bedroom's a bit disconcerting. Not just the pictures, her nightie's still hanging in his wardrobe. Yep. And all I

can talk about is 'sexual aids' in the cupboard under – i . . .
th . . . th . . . drawer under the bed, which I had to remove.
Oh yeah, mmmm. You know, vibrators and – KY Jelly and
stuff. And I just went berserk.

ROBERTA *laughs. The dog toy squeaks loudly.*

Went back to Christchurch, what do you think I'm going to
do? (*Laughs.*) Didn't like that very much. He said he didn't
know they were there; I said, 'Well, you should have
checked.' So. It's lovely, isn't it? It's a lovely garden, it's a
lovely house but it's all a bit . . . 'Nothing must be
changed.' You see, I don't like that – those three benches –
I know this sounds pathetic and childish, but there's loads of
pictures of Pauline pranc . . . sitting on those benches, and
he bought them for her. And he bought her the erm – bird –
bath, and he bought her the sundial. Hmm. Nice garden, we
have a lot of garden parties here.

11.

Collage (2'13")

ROY*'s house in the country.* ROBERTA *walks inside the
house, into the downstairs loo.*

ROBERTA. This is – this is – Roy's collage, mainly of . . .
These are nearly all Pauline, I think. Yeah, Pauline, that's
his wedding to Pauline. And. Most of them are Pauline,
I think. Oh, there's *me*. (*Laughs.*)

ROY (*entering*). Bobby's collage has gone back to Christchurch.

ROBERTA. Yes.

ROY. Following her latest stomp.

ROBERTA. Yes. I had a collage, and I put a lot of pictures of
boyfriends in cos . . .

ROY. And all the photographs went.

ROBERTA. Cos it annoyed me so much to have to – s . . . s . . .
He was gazing there at that every day, so I made my own
collage and / stuck it right in front of him.

ROY. / I wasn't 'gazing' at it . . . wasn't 'gazing' at it.

ROBERTA (*laughs*). And put lots of boyfriends in.

ROY. Darling, I've made the coffee, can you do the cups?

ROBERTA. Yes, dear.

    ROBERTA *exits to the kitchen.*

ROY. Come and – come and look at these photographs. This is – probably our main . . . You see, now . . . That's the centrepiece. A photograph of me – and Bobby, or Bobby and me / at uh – *at a Probus* – *at a Probus* . . .

ROBERTA (*re-entering*). / No, that's only just gone up there, that's Christmas.

ROY. Or is it a ladies' dinner night, love? / Was it Masonic? It must have been Masonic because of the bowtie. / And the DJ. / Yeah – yeah. A Masonic Ladies' Night. In the – local Trowbridge Civic Hall. And that's the centrepiece, now, of this display / – where there are probably of course . . .

ROBERTA. / Can't remember now. I can't –

ROBERTA. / mmmm / I put – I – I've rearranged the . . . I've rearranged these.

ROBERTA. / Well, err – You put it there. You put it there. I arrange the photos, and I always put myself right at the back – behind everything, because that's where I feel I am. I didn't put it there, he did it. That's after the . . . my last stomp. I think there was a sort of – (*Laughing.*)

ROY. 'Stomp'. Lovely word, isn't it?

ROBERTA. My 'last stomp'. / (*Laughing.*) And I came back, and he'd put that there / and I think that he 'd . . .

ROY. / She 'stomps' – / She 'stomps' with a certain, with a certain amount of *physical* presence.

ROBERTA (*laughs; opening a drawer*). They're all Pauline in there.

ROY (*laughing hard*). – Pauline. But I put them all in *here, you see.*

ROBERTA. They're all Pauline. These are all Pauline's that
I've put away. As I said, when I first came, they were
everywhere. Every single room you couldn't even have a
wee-wee in here without Pauline. (*Taking photos of Pauline
out of the drawer.*) . . . Pauline . . . *Pauline* . . . These were
all out – when I first came. I removed them.

ROY. It's good fun, isn't it? '*I* remove them. *I* remove them.'
And they're gradually coming back. (*Chuckles mischievously.*)
As she becomes . . . used to the idea. Come on. Coffee.

12.

Comments (2'37")

MAUREEN*'s living room. She reads from an A4 notebook.*

MAUREEN. This is – what I wrote about. I've written a
comment in all the people I've met. 'Colin: awful, nasty
habit' – cos he sort of kept on going (*She makes a snorting
noise and then starts laughing.*) like that. 'Don: not the
right type, ex-publican. Dave: yokel. Barry: too short, not
attractive. Alan: not the right class, nice-looking. Dave:
married. Brian: naughty but nice, gone to Spain. (*Laughing.*)
Michael: too poor.' – he was a nice chap, but he'd g . . .
hadn't got two ha'pennies to rub together. 'Richard: yes, but
lives too far' – he lived . . . lives in Morecambe. We're still
in touch, but . . . (*Coughs.*) And he's still married actually.
'Jack: short, big nose. (*Laughing.*) David: fat, Welsh.
Graham: no class, large family. Clive: too short, rich.' He's
actually the father of the one who owns Direct Dating,
and he put money into it. Yeah, so he is quite well off. Cos
they've got one-and-a-half million members now. Um
'Roger: bad type, sleazy. Bill: a nice man, don't fancy, but
will give him a chance.' Then I put: 'He didn't want it.'
(*Laughing.*) 'Michael: been around, handsome but no
property. Sexually flagging. Noel: nice friend – brackets
small lips. Twenty-seven, Roger: awful, common etcetera.'
erm and . . . Er . . . 'Twenty-nine, Peter: too fat. Thirty,
Gwilym: nice, but he doesn't seem interested in me.' Cos he
was one I really liked, I met him in Hay-on-Wye. – I quite

liked him. 'Peter: impotent, selfish. David:' – he was a nice one – 'super, sexy, but unreliable, not very tall.' He was about the same height as me. But he had – he . . . you know, he was too involved with other women, I think. He was that sort. And the last one Godfrey, another yokel. Never thought I'd meet so many without meeting Mr Right. I mean, I haven't slept with them all. No, because um . . . You know, I – I want to be in love, and . . . You know, I'm not interested otherwise, so . . .

13.

She'd Eat Me (1'32")

BERNARD*'s study.* BERNARD *sits at his desk and reads from his computer.*

BERNARD. 'Dating Direct dot com. New members in your area.' Okay? 'Hello Bernard, still single?' – 'Yes', uh . . . Right. Here we are. Carol. Now, I have to say – you know – she doesn't grab me. To be – honest, what does she have to say? Twyford? Oh, that's not bad. You see, that's within striking distance as far as I'm concerned. Widowed at thirty-*one*? Now, that *is* unusual. I mean, on this. So God knows – what she's been doing. Er . . . Now – this lady – *Maureen.* Um . . . (*Laughs.*) I think she'd eat me. (*Laughs, loudly.*) Yes. I'll tell you, I . . . uh . . . Within – well, when we'd got in touch – first by email, and then over the phone. She said, 'Oh, *do* come over for a weekend' and so on and so forth, 'and we'll have a lovely time, and then, you know, we'll go out to dinner – and when we come back w . . . you know, we can really . . . really go to town.' And, I mean, that . . . that was virtually what she was saying. I mean . . . (*Pause.*) Uh . . . She's, uh . . . (*Pause.*) Almost anxious, I . . . I would say – for a relationship. An I mean, that's a bit shapeless, isn't it?

14.

Dinner Dance (0'20")

MAUREEN*'s living room.*

MAUREEN. Oh yes – Bernard. We've spoken on the phone
two or three times and once or twice he's been going to
come up here and then he's called it off. An I asked him on
the internet if he'd like to come up and go as my partner to
a dinner dance and he said, 'Well, erm, yeah – I would like
to in principle but I don't know whether I can manage it.'

15.

Old Dog (0'58")

DUDLEY*'s flat.*

DUDLEY. Yeah, I'll try not a cough. Uh. I met a lady – from a
dating agency – that come from Leominster. But – eh –
nothing progressed out o that. And then I came off the
dating agency.

We weren't really compatible. I mean, it – sometimes you
meet somebody and it's . . . It happens, dun it? And other
times, it's 'Oh, I don't want that.' (*Laughs.*) So, there we go.
I mean, there's still life in the old dog – yet, you know.

Pause.

She did tell me she was still in love with her – ex-boyfriend.
He was a millionaire. So I got no chance. (*Laughs and
coughs.*) Cos I'm no millionaire. (*Laughs.*) I think you
might know her. I got an idea you might know her.

He laughs. There is a pause.

Do ya?

16.

Sophisticated (0'15")

MAUREEN*'s living room.*

MAUREEN. You can – understand probably why I didn't think
he was the man for me. (*Laughs.*) I – I met him, a couple of
times. Erm, well, maybe three times, but, you know, he
wasn't really sophisticated enough for me.

17.

Prince Rupert (0'49")

PETER*'s living room.*

PETER. We met at – Shrewsbury, at the Prince Rupert. And –
when I got there, this lady was walking towards me. One
look – (*He makes a whooshing sound.*) God. No way. Took
all of two seconds to make me mind up about that one. But
I had – said that we would meet for lunch, and I was hungry
even if she wasn't. So I thought, 'Sod it, I'm having lunch.'
So we had a bar snack – in the bar. On . . . settee. Bit like
that one. And during the course of lunch, she pointed to me
stomach – and poked it. And she says, 'I wouldn't like to
think of that being on top of me.' (*Laughing.*) I nearly said
to her, 'Don't worry, you ain't gonna get the chance.'
(*Laughs.*)

18.

Huge Chap (0'22")

MAUREEN*'s living room.*

MAUREEN. He was a bit cross with me when I told him he
was too fat. (*Laughs.*) I mean, I didn't say it like that – I
didn't say 'You're too fat', but I . . . I did say, you know –
I – 'Maybe you ought to lose a bit of weight', but I did say
'Well, I do too actually', you know, but he didn't like it. But
he was a huge chap. I couldn't fancy him.

19.

Good-Looking Professional Male (1'11")

PETER*'s living room. He reads from a file.*

PETER. I am a good-looking, professional person. I live on my own – with a dog. I am looking for a good-looking lady, with whom I could share life and grow old gracefully. I definitely do – *not* – want – one-night stands. This is a very serious approach to try and develop a lasting partnership based on mutual trust, committed love – and affection. If you are happy to laugh with me, to hold hands, to hug and to kiss – to share happiness, and the occasional bit of sadness when it arises, then do please contact me. All I ask is openness on *both* our parts, and the courtesy of a reply to my approaches. It was – bout ten days before we, erm . . . uh . . . Anna turned up. She . . . is . . . pretty – nice. She's quite smoking, actually. I think that one's going to go at a fair speed, so . . . (*A sigh, he rubs his hands together.*) Ah . . . find the Viagra. (*Laughs.*)

20.

Past It (1'55")

MAUREEN*'s living room.*

MAUREEN. Cos I've got this little friend Margaret, who's seventy-six – actually. Three years ago she met a chap on a cruise. Who lived in, um – way over the other side. Norfolk way. And, um. You know, she was really very keen on him. And – they didn't have sex, because. Well, she reckoned that – she said – she . . . and I mean I p . . . I think it's a load of rubbish, she said, 'He respects me (*Laughing.*) too much.' And I mean – he ei . . . he's about eighty-four, but you know. Good for his age. And, ah – I said, well, there's something funny, you know, because if he really – if he . . . sh . . . I said, 'Probably he's past it.' She said, 'Oh no, he definitely isn't past it, because I can feel that when he holds me (*Laughing.*) close.' (*Laughs loudly.*)

She has got two other men friends that she's met on cruises. Um because, she's met Jack – who's a very good dancer, and he's eight . . . bout eighty-two. And, um, she goes with him on dancing holidays. And cos she's a bronze medallist. And she's got, um a pacemaker. Yeah.

And then, um. Geoff, she met on – uh – she went on a cruise. Was it last – um – no . . . Yes . . . end of . . . May – she met him on a cruise, and he lives in Shrewsbury. And he . . . he's only seventy-*eight*. (*Laughs.*) And, um, he's very keen on her, and he comes over a lot, and she goes over to him. And she's not so keen on him, she likes him – but, you know, that's all. She likes him as a friend. But he – he'd be interested in rather more. So he was very pleased when it was all finished with this 'Jim'. And he said, 'Oh, one down, one to go.' (*Laughs.*)

21.

Chat-Up Line and Chaperone (1'36")

MARGARET's *bungalow.*

MARGARET. His chat-up line was: 'I've had a gin and tonic, and two glasses of red wine,' um, 'would you like to dance?'

MARGARET *and* GEOFF *laugh.*

So, I thought, 'Well – it can only get better.'

They laugh again.

GEOFF. Actually it got worse, didn't it?

MARGARET. It did, he kept bumping in to people.

GEOFF. Yeah. She said, 'You dance better when you've had two gin and (*Laughing.*) tonics and two gi . . . two glasses of wine.' (*Laughs. Pause.*) Well, she wouldn't come – wouldn't come up to my place without Maureen.

MARGARET. Well / – I . . .

GEOFF. / Well, I mean – I asked her if she wanted to come up to my place for the weekend . . .

MARGARET. No.

GEOFF. . . . and she says, 'No, not on my own.'

MARGARET. It was to go to a concert, wasn't it, in a church?

GEOFF. Yeah. Urm. She says, 'No, not on my own.'

MARGARET. Ah no, I said, 'Can I bring a friend?' You said, 'Yes, as long as it's not a man.'

>MARGARET *and* GEOFF *laugh heartily.*

GEOFF. Then she had r . . . then . . . then she had to sort of fine . . . find someone that . . . who would come with her.

MARGARET. And I thought fancy picking Maureen because without a hearing aid we could have been – playing – all night, you know. (*They laugh.*) She wouldn't have heard a sound. I thought, what a . . .

>MARGARET *and* GEOFF *laugh heartily.*

>What a person to choose – as my chaperone. / Somebody who won't hear a noise.

GEOFF. / Yeah . . . Yeah.

MARGARET. But as he was so well-behaved, I didn't take Maureen the next time. Thought I could trust him. Didn't I?

GEOFF. Oh yes, oh yes, I mean. (*Pause.*) Can't do much otherwise when you're eighty.

>MARGARET *and* GEOFF *laugh.*

MARGARET. Well, let's just say we're playing it very slowly.

GEOFF. Yeah.

MARGARET. Yes, yes. I mean, what's the rush really – (*Laughing.*) at our age as he said.

GEOFF. That's right, yeah.

>*Silence.*

22.

Very Keen (0'41")

MAUREEN's *living room.*

MAUREEN. When time goes on – and – we're all – you know, the older age group, the women get all keen and interested again, and the men are flagging and . . . (*Laughing.*) can't oblige. Well, I mean, that's why I feel I need a younger man, because – when they get to about seventy, they've had it. Yeah but whereas women have st . . . Women can carry on till they die. The menopause very often makes women – *more* so. But *men* – um er – a lot of men have prostate problems, and that kills it dead. A lot of those I've met on the . . . They still want to have a woman for company, but they can't perform – and a lot of them take Viagra.

23.

Bath Towel (2'22")

PETER's *living room.*

PETER. But there's a new one out now, that's called Cialis. And it's known as 'The Weekend – Pill'. Because it lasts – for longer than – Viagra. So that if you miss out on the first night, you've still got enough left in your body for the next night. And maybe *even* the night after. Mmm. Er – th . . . this one over at Tamworth – I used to turn her inside out. Oh yes, she . . . she . . . she was absolute – ooh. She was *hot*. She was a *nympho*. It got to the stage ver . . . fairly quickly – where – um – I just was totally in . . . unable to . . . to er – perform any form of satisfaction myself. This was even with the Viagra. And so, it was – er – a quick trip to Ann Summers. I . . . I got erm . . . a . . . a . . . fairly – hefty-sized dildo. And um . . . a few appropriate creams. And er . . . finished her off that way.

The effect was *such* – and you'll have to pardon this one – but we had to have a bath towel underneath her. *Yes*. I – at that time, did not *know* that a female could ejaculate. But apparently there are two glands either side, that – if they're given the right simu . . . stimulation, will pour forth (*Laughing.*) copious quantities. (*Laughs.*) Yeah. And she – ooh, she used to flood the place. (*Laughing.*) Yeah – it squirted out. (*Laughs.*) All over me. (*Laughs.*) It really was – it was funny because it was . . . (*Laughs, he makes a whooshing water sound accompanied by thrusting actions.*) like this. Oh God it was – 'Me arm's tired' – have a rest. (*He starts the thrusting actions again.*) And she'd just be – moaning, and . . . 'Ooh' . . . all the rest of it, you know. (*Laughing.*) And r . . . really sort of, in another world. And, er, afterwards she'd just turn over, and she'd be sssnoring her head off, and she'd have the best night's sleep she'd had in years. (*Laughs.*)

24.

Leftovers (1'30")

MARGARET*'s bungalow.*

GEOFF. I dated two – two ladies from 'Kindred Spirits' in the *Daily Telegraph.* And I got the completely wrong impression. I mean, course, these things in the *Telegraph* – I mean they . . . People tell such lies.

MARGARET *laughs first and then* GEOFF *joins in.*

MARGARET. Oh you are naïve – You are naïve. / Poor little thing.

GEOFF. / And this woman, she um – I mean, it said it would . . . erm . . . She was tall, um, dark-haired, medium build or something or other. Well, I mean, she was tall, but medium build she certainly *wasn't.* And, uh, I . . . I . . . I'm not, sort of, disposed towards fat women.

MARGARET *is laughing in the background.*

And uh. She'd worked all her life in catering. And then . . . then she went into, um. She got a job as a um, a cook for a school. Well, I think she must have eaten all the leftovers.

Because she was *big*. But uh, I mean, then again – I . . . I . . . I thought, 'Well, this isn't going to work', because – I . . . I . . . I talked about holidays that I did and uh, you know – well, since my wife died, five years ago, I'd been on two, three, sometimes four holidays in a year – and she was like 'Oh, you are lucky,' she says. 'I wish I could afford a holiday', and I thought, 'Uh-oh.'

He laughs and MARGARET *joins in loudly.*

MARGARET. You find that the men like the women who can pay for themselves.

GEOFF. Yeah. Yeah. Well, I was looking for a rich widow, but I didn't find one.

25.

Bernard's Quite Keen Now (0'14")

MAUREEN's *living room.*

MAUREEN. I think Bernard is quite keen now. An he was trying to get me when I was away. Erm because I sent him that photo and he said he thought that photo was much nicer than the other ones that were on – on the dating thing.

26.

Come Down and See Me (0'10")

BERNARD's *study.*

BERNARD. We exchanged an e-mail or two and Maureen said you know 'W – would you like to come down and see me?' And I thought, 'Well, you know, it's fine.'

27.

University (0'13")

MAUREEN's *living room.*

MAUREEN. This is Bernard – so he looks quite nice, doesn't he? See, he went to university. (*Reading from* BERNARD's *printed profile.*) 'I have great health, energy and vitality, I'm told that I look and act years younger than my age, and I'm smart and amusing – '

28.

An Old Romantic (0'12")

BERNARD's *study. Reading from his online profile.*

BERNARD. ' – for sure. I have a good sense of humour, I'm well travelled and enjoy holidays in this country and many others – err I'm probably a romantic at heart – '

29.

A Lady to Please (0'05")

MAUREEN's *living room. Continues reading from his printed profile.*

MAUREEN. ' – certainly I'm a tactile, loving man and I want a lady to please and cherish.' I would like to meet him.

30.

On Trial (0'44")

MARGARET's *bungalow.*

MARGARET. Well, we'll ask you to the wedding if it happens. That was joke. That was joke. (*Pause.*) Wasn't it. That was a joke, wasn't it, Geoff?

GEOFF. Yes . . . No, no.

MARGARET. Ah no, he's not going to let me.

MARGARET *and* GEOFF *laugh.*

You say – you say it.

GEOFF. Ask us after the July cruise. (*Laughs.*)

MARGARET. There's a lot hanging on this – on this cruise, is there? I think I'm on trial or something.

GEOFF. Aren't we both?

MARGARET. Yes, we're both on trial at the moment.

GEOFF. I mean, we both – both of us w . . . would have to make sacrifices. If we, uh –

MARGARET. Well, I'm not going to make any. (*Laughs.*)

GEOFF. Well, that's your answer, isn't it then? (*Laughs.*)

31.

Rebound (0'54")

MAUREEN*'s living room.*

MAUREEN. About Margaret and, uh, *Geoff* – you know, I think she's – happy to get married to him, but I don't think she's in love with him. Because – um, you know she was, um – given the runaround by somebody else who only – dumped her a little while ago. For somebody else. So it's . . . I think it's a bit on the rebound. But h . . . he's a nice chap, you know, and he's got plenty of money. So, um, you know, I think she's . . . you know, she thought yes, she . . . she would – but I don't know whether she's considered the financial implications and I'm – taking her a little gift and a card, but I'm also taking her a very good article to read, which I kept – in case I ever got married again. A lot of people in our age group *don't* get married because of the finances – for one thing, I don't know wha . . . You see, I don't know whether she's thought about it but this article – I'll . . . *Alert* her.

32.

The Rumba (2'10")

MARGARET's *bungalow.*

GEOFF *and* MARGARET *rumba to 'Where Do I Begin' by Shirley Bassey.*

33.

Congratulations! (9'56")

MARGARET's *bungalow.*

GEOFF *is humming a jaunty tune.* MAUREEN *arrives at the front door with a gift bag.*

MAUREEN. Hello? Hellerr?

MARGARET. Good good good.

> MAUREEN *chuckles.*

How are you?

MAUREEN. That's an engagement present, but if Geoff's got one, I'll take it back. I don't know whether he's got one.

MARGARET. Have you got one?

MAUREEN. Er – well, you've got to look and see what it is. And / there's a . . .

MARGARET. / Thank you very much.

MAUREEN. . . . a very good article there about the financial implications of two people getting married again.

MARGARET. Oh.

MAUREEN. It tells you all the – pros and / cons . . .

GEOFF. / Money? Don't worry. (*Laughs.*)

MAUREEN. Yeah, no. Pension's / very important.

GEOFF. / How are you?

MAUREEN. Very well, thank you.

GEOFF *laughs*.

Yeah, card.

MARGARET. Oh – thank you very much. That was . . . that was quick.

GEOFF *laughs*.

MAUREEN. It's not . . . not a proper engagement card. / It's just an ordinary card. (*Laughs.*)

MARGARET. / Thank you very much – come in, please – please.

MAUREEN. Yes – congratulations.

GEOFF. Thank you very much (*Laughs.*)

MARGARET. / Ooh.

MAUREEN. / It's an electric one.

GEOFF. What's that?

MARGARET. Have you got one of those?

MAUREEN. An electric pepper mill.

GEOFF. No. / No.

MAUREEN. / Oh good. You've not / got one. Right.

GEOFF. / No. Oh, no.

MAUREEN. / There you are.

MARGARET. / Thank you / Maureen.

GEOFF. / Thank you very much. Thank you.

MARGARET. That's great, / isn't it?

GEOFF. / Mmm. Yes.

MARGARET. No, I haven't got one either.

MAUREEN. Well, yeah, I saw somebody using one in Germany, and I thought it was so good, and I looked there – they were very expensive there . . . I saw them here in Woolies.

MARGARET *and* MAUREEN *laugh.*

Yeah.

MARGARET (*to audience*). She's a scream, isn't she?

MAUREEN (*sits on the sofa*). Ah, one thing . . .

MARGARET (*reading from the card*). 'Dear Margaret and Geoff, / my sincerest wishes. Hope you have a wonderful time and life together.'

MAUREEN. / Yeah.

MARGARET. That's lovely – thank you very much, Maureen.

MAUREEN. Er, one thing I wanted to ask you is, what was your son's reaction?

MARGARET. My son? He said, 'Blimey.'

MARGARET *laughs.*

We told the – asked the vicar this morning to keep it free.

MAUREEN. And he's . . . they've got a vacancy?

MARGARET. What?

MAUREEN. Well, in . . . very often, churches get booked up on Saturdays.

GEOFF. / Oh yes.

MARGARET. / Yes yes. But he phoned up and said / that was okay.

MAUREEN. / Yeah.

GEOFF. / Oh well. They'd cancel everything for . . . for us.

MAUREEN. And it's for better or for worse.

MARGARET (*laughing*). Oh, Maureen.

MARGARET, GEOFF *and* MAUREEN *are all laughing.*

MAUREEN. So . . .

GEOFF. Yeah – certainly for – richer and poorer.

MAUREEN. Yeah. Yeah yeah yeah.

MARGARET. Oh God. Oh.

MAUREEN. I'm not . . . As I uh – Margaret probably told you, I was surprised . . . I wasn't surprised that you asked her, but I was surprised that she said 'Yes'. Yeah.

MAUREEN *laughs as* GEOFF *harrumphs.*

Well, because you know . . . she always said, 'Oh, I'm not going to get married again, it's much more sensible to live with somebody.' You did.

GEOFF. Well, I . . . I always / say you should . . .

MARGARET. / Yeah. Yeah. I probably did.

MAUREEN. Yeah . . .

GEOFF. / Well . . .

MARGARET. / I probably . . . I probably . . .

MAUREEN (*continuing*). . . . because if you . . . if you do split up – when you're married, it's more difficult. / Um.

MARGARET. / We're not . . . we're not planning on 'splitting up'.

MAUREEN. No, I know. Nobody does though, do they? I'm only thinking of you . . . I told you about my aromatherapist – no – acupuncturist, and *her* mother got married again, and then after two years . . . They, you know, they split up.

MARGARET. Well . . . Not all do.

MAUREEN. Yeah. No no, but I . . . it happens.

MARGARET. Oh well, Maureen . . .

MAUREEN *laughs.*

GEOFF. Two guidelines – there are two guidelines in . . . / life.

MAUREEN. / Yes.

GEOFF. Never be positive – on anything.

MAUREEN. Yeah.

GEOFF. And never burn bridges.

Pause.

MAUREEN. Never burn bridges?

GEOFF. Mmm.

MAUREEN. Oh, I think you should burn all your bridges. (*Laughs.*)

GEOFF. No. Never burn / bridges.

MAUREEN. / Yeah. Mmm.

GEOFF. You might wanna . . . Track back . . .

MAUREEN. Yeah. (*Laughs politely.*)

GEOFF. / . . . and never be positive . . .

MAUREEN. / Are you keeping your house on then, / up there?

GEOFF. / Sorry?

MAUREEN. Are you keeping your house on in Shropshire?

GEOFF. No.

MAUREEN. Oh. Well, you're burning your bridge there / then.

GEOFF. / No I'm not.

Pause.

No, I'm not really. I . . . Well, I mean, burning bridges I'm re . . . I . . . I . . . I refer – mainly to uh – friendships.

MAUREEN. Oh, right. / Oh no, I agree there.

GEOFF. / I mean, I know people who say, 'Well, I'm never going to speak to them again.'

MAUREEN. Yeah, yeah.

Pause.

I've already decided I'll be able to wear the suit I wore at Caroline's wedding – cos I haven't worn it since. So it'll / be an . . . a little outing for it.

MARGARET. / Oh, that'll be nice. I was thinking of wearing the one that I wore for Simon's wedding.

MAUREEN. Oh well, / why not?

GEOFF. / Oh well, I'm pleased I'll have something new.

MAUREEN. Yeah, why not?

MARGARET. It's a suit. Quite a short skirt. Little jacket. And a great big hat. All the same colour. And there's a blouse that goes / with it that's exactly the same colour.

GEOFF. / Do short skirts suit you?

MARGARET. Pardon?

GEOFF. Does a short skirt suit you?

Pause.

MARGARET. What's wrong with *my* legs? / Well, you haven't really s . . .

GEOFF. / Well, no – I . . . I . . . I'm just saying.

MAUREEN *laughs.*

I'm not – I . . . I . . . I'm not criticising, I'm just – asking.

MARGARET. / No, it . . . It's a long jacket and a short skirt. You . . .

GEOFF. / I'm only asking . . . You . . . A . . . a . . . a mature woman. Mature women in short skirts sometimes look a bit odd.

Pause.

At least I'll have something new.

MAUREEN *laughs.*

MARGARET. Are you going to get a suit? (*Laughs.*)

GEOFF. Well, I'll buy a new suit.

MAUREEN. Yeah.

GEOFF. Always find an ex . . . always like an excuse for buying – clothes.

Pause.

I rather fancy a nice – c . . . pale-coloured suit with matching shoes.

GEOFF *gets up and gets the champagne.*

MAUREEN *laughs.*

This is what we were use . . . drinking yesterday.

He exits to the kitchen with the champagne.

MAUREEN. Ah. Hmm. Have you told Jack yet?

MARGARET. No.

MAUREEN. Ah. Poor old Jack.

MARGARET. Well, he was rabbitting on about it all . . . all Christmas, about when I was going to marry . . . and I came – 'For goodness' sakes, stop . . . ah . . . just. Shut up about it.' This is my dancing partner that I went to . . . to, um, Vienna with. Um. Before things had (*Laughing.*) warmed up here. (*Laughs.*) I got fed up with him.

MAUREEN. But anyway she's got a dancing holiday booked with Geoff, and she's still going / on it.

MARGARET. / Jack . . . With Jack.

MAUREEN. Jack, rather.

MARGARET. Yes.

MAUREEN. I've never heard of anybody else's fiancée going away with another man, have you? No. (*Laughs.*)

MARGARET. But it's just the way it's happened.

MAUREEN. Yeah.

MARGARET. I mean, I was surprised. He . . . He – seemed to be including me in . . . in all the – thoughts about a house, you see. And I thought, 'That's funny, he hasn't said anything.'

She laughs. GEOFF *hums in the background.*

So I said, 'Have you forgotten something?' and he said erm – 'What do you mean?', and I said, 'You haven't asked me if I want to live with you.' He said, 'Oh I'm s . . . ' – he said, 'I've been taking you for granted', and then he asked me to marry him.

A cork pops.

GEOFF. Ooh – ah.

MAUREEN *chuckles politely.*

MARGARET. But he's a bit cagey tonight.

GEOFF. Should have done it in here.

MARGARET. Why?

GEOFF. Popped it in here, but it . . .

MARGARET. What have you hit?

GEOFF. No, I said I should have popped it in here, / but uh . . . It . . .

MAUREEN. / Oh, you didn't want to have a – dribbles on the carpet. Cheers, / cheers.

MARGARET. / Thank you very much.

GEOFF. Thank you.

GEOFF *and* MAUREEN. Cheers.

MARGARET. Cheers. (*Laughs.*)

A hearing aid begins to whistle.

MAUREEN. 'Scuse me.

MARGARET. Oh.

MAUREEN. Oh, I don't know whether you get this happen.

GEOFF. Oh, what's that, condensation?

MAUREEN. Condensation.

GEOFF. Mmm.

MAUREEN *takes out her hearing aid and blows in it. The whistling stops.*

MAUREEN. That's it. I think, 'Oh, I hope it doesn't   happen when I'm with a gentleman.'

GEOFF *laughs.*

/ It hasn't so far, but –

GEOFF. / No – you've got a / – hot ear (*Laughs.*)

MARGARET (*laughing*). / He'll think he's pressing your buttons, Maureen.

MARGARET, GEOFF *and* MAUREEN *are all laughing.*

MAUREEN. Ooh, look at this, ooh.

MARGARET. It's just a little cheesy scone.

GEOFF. We told Joan last night, we wondered how quickly it would get round.

MARGARET. Poor Joan, she's got . . . Her eyebrows hit . . . hit the roof.

MAUREEN. Really?

MARGARET. She kept saying . . . What was it she kept saying? 'You could have – popped me down with a feather', or something.

GEOFF. Mmm. Yeah.

MAUREEN. No, well – I was surprised. Because, uh – no . . . I didn't think you would. (*Laughs.*)

There is a pause.

MARGARET. Well, I mean . . .

GEOFF. We're not all like you, you know, we don't sort of think – well, you know – s . . . see how many we can – you know . . .

MARGARET. No, but . . .

MAUREEN. Now, / don't make assumptions.

GEOFF. / . . . Choose from . . .

GEOFF *laughs.*

MARGARET. / No, as I . . . as I said . . .

MAUREEN. / No but I . . . I . . . I mean, I've known Margaret
longer than you have, so I know what she's said to me in
the past, so.

GEOFF. See, all I've gotta be careful of, is that – you know,
when . . . when the knot is tied, that – within seconds I've
got to sign my will. (*Laughs.*)

MAUREEN. Well, that's one of the things in that article, /
you've both got – you've *both* got to make new wills.

MARGARET. / That's something . . . that's what . . .

GEOFF. Mmm.

MARGARET. Well, / we just found that out today, actually.

MAUREEN. / Because when you get married it negates any
will that you've made.

GEOFF. That's right.

MARGARET. Yes, well, we just found that out today. His
friend, um . . .

MAUREEN. Really?

MARGARET. Yes.

GEOFF. Yeah. Mmm.

MAUREEN. Well, you see, I'm quite up, you know – I'm quite
knowledgeable about these things because I get this . . .
from the *Saga* magazine, *Choice*, and *Yours* – and they've
always these articles about it. / So, and they say yes, um –
I mean . . . that one . . .

MARGARET. / Oh right.

MAUREEN. . . . . it's a little bit dated, but most of it's – still
relevant . . .

MARGARET. Thank you, / Maureen.

MAUREEN. / . . . But, I mean, one of the things is about
pension – I . . . Do you still get your husband's pension
when you get married?

MARGARET. Well, I don't know, / do I?

MAUREEN. / No, well, you see, you may not. Most companies don't, my husband's company *does* – / pay the pension . . .

MARGARET. / Oh yes, that's a thought . . .

MAUREEN. . . . . Then – then – does . . . does Geoff's company – supposing he pre-deceases you – and you have lost your co . . . your pension from Roy c – does Geoff's company pay you, probably not because they don't usually give a pension to a wife after the man's retired. (*Pause.*) In fact it said you should consult a financial advisor . . .

GEOFF. Oh / no, I don't like financial . . .

MAUREEN. / . . . Because you could be worse off if you lost Roy's pension and then you married Geoff, and then you didn't . . . you didn't get any pension through Geoff.

Pause. MAUREEN *clears her throat.*

MARGARET. That's true.

MAUREEN. That's why some people don't get married, because of losing the pension.

A long pause.

MARGARET. Mmm, mmmm. I didn't – well, I – I mean, it sounded simple the way we thought it out, didn't it?

GEOFF. Yeah.

MARGARET. But then there are all these little – laws that you don't know about. I'll get onto them.

MAUREEN *chuckles.*

Find all the ins and outs.

MAUREEN. Yeah. (*Pause.*) But I mean, Margaret / *hasn't at least –*

GEOFF *gets up from his chair.*

– oh oh oh.

MARGARET. / Ooh. Ooh. (*Falling off the arm of* GEOFF*'s chair.*)

MAUREEN *laughs uncontrollably.*

GEOFF. What? What happened?

MAUREEN. The chair tipped up when / you got off it.

GEOFF. / Oh, that's all right.

MARGARET, GEOFF *and* MAUREEN *laugh.*

MARGARET. Oh dear. If it's going to be like that. Ohh.

MAUREEN. Make sure he doesn't take out a big insurance on you. (*Laughs.*)

MARGARET (*laughing*). Oh dear. Oh dear. Oh Maureen, what a thing to say.

34.

Ordinary Chap (0'50")

MAUREEN'*s living room.*

MAUREEN. I've spoken with a lot of her friends, and everybody says, 'Ooh, you know' – and um, 'She's taking a big step there', and . . . Mainly because – Margaret's enjoyed her freedom, since her husband died. I think he was quite dictatorial. I think she was quite – flirtatious and flighty, you know. So he had to keep her a bit like that. (*Mimes under the thumb action. Laughs.*) Yeah. I mean, at the moment Margaret is being very – sort of – very prim, but, you know, basically she's not like that. (*Laughs.*) She might find that she gets a bit bored. Geoff's just an ordinary – ordinary chap, isn't he? Time alone will tell, because she likes excitement, and I mean, she's not going to get it there.

35.

Jim, Jack and Geoff (1'30")

MARGARET'*s bungalow.*

MARGARET. I was very keen on somebody else when I first met him. Well, about two years before I met Geoff, I met

this very nice man, very charming – on a cruise. This is Jim.
Romance blossomed a bit, you know, it was a holiday
atmosphere, you know how it is. Um, nothing as mundane
as the rest of life, and then, um, we were going on a cruise –
last – autumn, and by this time, I'd met Geoff and I'd also
met my dancing partner on a previous cruise. The dancing
partner has no romance in it at all, we're just very good
friends, and he's an *extremely* good dancer – and though
I say it myself, I am too. And, uh, Jack and I got along fine
so I (*Laughing.*) got Geoff, Jack and . . . No, Jim, Geo . . .
Jack and Geoff, you see – which kept confusing people. Cos
one of them, when Jack turned up, wh . . . uh – when Geoff
turned up, people started calling him Jack. (*Laughs.*)

And I'm still very friendly with Jack, and he's coming to
the wedding. We . . . well, that last cruise with Jim, about
the second night out he said, um – that he'd found some
woman who was twenty years younger than he was, and he
was thinking of spending the rest of his life with her. And
I thought, 'Okay mate, you do that', you know. Cos it didn't
bother me at all, then. (*Laughs.*) Because I . . . because I'd
already met Geoff, and I thought, well, you know – 'This is
very nice', and he was – much nearer, and we saw a lot
of each other. And he's good company. H . . . he just
(*Laughs.*) – I wouldn't like to say he wore me down, but
he was very persistent.

36.

Moon and the Stars (0'24")

MAUREEN*'s living room.*

MAUREEN. Bernard phoned last night – so he's uh coming –
    not this weekend, but the next weekend – all being well.
    He reckons I've promised him the moon and the stars.
    (*Laughs.*) But, the thing is, of course, he's a man who is
    getting on in his years, and he won't have a lot of time left.
    None of them have at that time . . . an I mean, I hate Viagra.

37.

Expectations (0'09")

BERNARD*'s study.*

BERNARD. We both had expectations. I think, I think she's
eat – (*Laughs.*) a gentleman friend. (*Laughs raucously.*)

During MAUREEN*'s next speech,* BERNARD, *in high
spirits, sings 'Lullaby of Broadway' as he packs his bag for
his visit.*

38.

Wedding Outfits (0'46")

MAUREEN*'s living room.*

MAUREEN (*on the phone*). So anyway, I hope that it does
come off because, you know . . . as you know, I've met a
lot of men, but he's – *really* the first one that I've felt was
absolutely right. I told Margaret and Geoff – they met me
when I came back from Dorchester and I had a meal with
them. And, do you know, I think she was a bit premature,
they've sent the wedding invitations out already – so many
months in advance. An, and they've bought their wedding
outfits as well. (*Laughs.*) They went to some – um – big
factory shop near Walsall that sells designer things at
discounted prices. I – I mean, I think she's crazy really,
I have to say. But anyway, it may work out. Who knows?

39.

Charisma (3'10")

MARGARET*'s bungalow.* MAUREEN *arrives at the front
door.* MARGARET *and* GEOFF *are in the living room.*

MAUREEN. Hello.

MARGARET. Come in, come in.

MAUREEN. You're sitting watching television looking like the old married couple.

MARGARET. No, we're – No, we're just having a chat / actually.

MAUREEN. / Oh right, oh right.

MARGARET. Here's Geoffrey.

MAUREEN. Hello.

GEOFF. How are you?

MAUREEN. Very well, thank you. / Good, yeah.

MARGARET. / Have you seen my engagement ring?

MAUREEN. Yeah, yes. / (*Laughs.*) Yes I've seen it, yeah – yeah.

MARGARET. / Isn't it pretty?

MARGARET. Get it in a good light, / dear, it's . . .

MAUREEN. / Cos last time we were here we were talking about it, weren't we?

MARGARET. Isn't / it pretty?

MAUREEN. / Yeah. Mmm. Chose it together? Yeah. / Mmm. You chose it together, presumably? /

MARGARET. / Sorry? / Oh, yes yes yes.

MAUREEN. But not at the, um – 'reduced items' place.

MARGARET *laughs, and then* MAUREEN *joins in.*

MARGARET. I don't know, it's – I don't know where he *suggested* going, but . . .

MAUREEN. You don't wear your wedding . . . your original wedding ring?

MARGARET. Pardon?

MAUREEN. You don't wear your original / wedding ring?

MARGARET. / No. No. Well, I'm not married, am I?

MAUREEN. Oh, you are when you're a widow, you still wear your rings. I've / always worn mine.

GEOFF. / I don't wear mine. Don't wear mine.

MAUREEN. But widows wear their rings.

GEOFF. / No.

MAUREEN. / Yeah.

MARGARET. Well, I just decided that, if I got an engagement ring, that's what I would wear.

GEOFF. Yeah.

MARGARET. Mmmm.

Pause.

I mean, this is . . .

GEOFF. Off with the old and on with the new. / Isn't it?

MARGARET. / Well, this is the start of something different, / isn't it?

GEOFF. / Yeah. That's right, you don't want any . . . all the old ghosts about, do we?

MARGARET. No. I'm very happy with what I have.

MAUREEN. Good.

GEOFF. Oh good. You won't get another one, so you'd better be.

MARGARET, GEOFF *and* MAUREEN *laugh.*

MAUREEN. Anyway, how is Jack? (*Laughs lightly.*)

MARGARET. He's fine.

MAUREEN. Yeah.

MARGARET. Yes, he's very well. (*Pause.*) In fact I've . . . I – this is my dancing partner, who is eighty-two, and very spry.

MAUREEN. Bernard, the one from Bournemouth's coming up to stay with me next weekend. / Not this weekend, / next weekend.

MARGARET. / Ooh. / Right. That'll be nice, / what are you going to do with him?

MAUREEN. / We have been, uh – keeping in touch.

MARGARET. Going to take him anywhere?

MAUREEN. Erm, well, I say that if I go to the, um Talgarth Male Boys Choir, / he'll have to come with me there . . .

MARGARET. / Oh, that'll be nice. That'll be nice.

MAUREEN. . . . because I'm helping with the refreshments. / And Bernard has David's charisma. (*Laughs, naughtily.*) /

MARGARET. / Good. / Well, I hope that's all of Bern . . . of David's he's got.

MAUREEN. Well, I mean, I know that you and David didn't like each other, but most people found David quite charismatic.

MARGARET. Really?

MAUREEN. Yeah. / Even your friend, um – /

MARGARET. / Oh. / Mary?

MAUREEN. Sorry?

MARGARET. Mary?

MAUREEN. Mary, yes, she said she thought David was very nice. Mmm.

MARGARET. Well, I mean, he was very charming, to order, / wasn't he?

MAUREEN. / Yeah, that's right, he knows how to be charming / . . .

MARGARET. / Yes.

MAUREEN. . . . but he had the – I mean, he definitely had charisma because I saw it on the cruises, the way all the ladies just, sort of – you know – fell for him.

MARGARET. Well, he put himself out / to be . . .

MAUREEN. / Sorry?

MARGARET. He put himself out to be pleasant / and people used to react to that.

MAUREEN. / Well, that's right. Well, that was his . . . / That was . . . yeah –

MARGARET. / But I mean, if it . . . It's all very well being pleasant, but I mean . . . I'd think a bit of sincerity would have been nice too. (*Laughs.*)

MAUREEN. Well, yes that's true, but erm . . . People don't – I mean, I just . . . I . . . The sort of man I fall for, the ones who are extremely charismatic. (*Laughs.*)

MARGARET. Yes. Well. Let's hope that / – you get one with a bit more charis –

MAUREEN. / Yeah.

MAUREEN *laughs gently. There is a brief pause.*

Hmmm.

Silence. MAUREEN *takes a crisp and eats.*

40.

Stopping Dating (1'22")

MAUREEN'*s living room.*

MAUREEN. After Bernard, I'm not going to bother to make . . . to bother at all. I'm stopping dating, I've had enough – three years. I mean, I have a full life I w – I had a good time at the weekend. Saturday I went with one friend . . . we went to Llandovery and I bought a lovely skirt – oh, I'll show it you and then we went to Aberdovey on Monday. And urm yeah, you know, I just can't be bothered meeting all these rubbishy men any more, so many of them are rubbish. (*Laughs.*) When you think, you know – after David – Bernard's the first one that I've really felt worth pursuing. (*Laughs.*) You know, I . . . he might not think the same about me, so . . . But I mean, I think he assumes that we will – sleep together. And I suppose I will – because it's been such a long time. You know, I'm (*Laughing.*) quite keen, really. But he might – he might *only* he interested in that, and then it makes you feel cheap. I mean, if he comes up, and – you know, we sleep together and then he goes back and then I never see him again, I'll think, 'Oh, why did I?', you know. It's the same, you see, at my age – seventy-two – as at thirty-two. You know, it's still – a problem, except that you know in your generation, everybody – expects it. Very difficult.

41.

The Vows (2'24")

The Priory Church, Leominster.

FATHER. . . . Silence is the best response to that.

> *Soft laughter in the congregation.*

We can now continue. The vows that you are about to take, are to be made in the presence of God, who is judge of all, and who knows *all* the secrets of our hearts. Therefore if either of *you* knows a reason – why you may not *lawfully* marry, you must declare it now.

Pause.

Geoff, will you take – Margaret to be your wife? Will you love her, comfort her, honour and protect her, and forsaking *all* others, be faithful to her – as long as you both shall live?

GEOFF. I will.

FATHER. And Margaret, will you take Geoff to be your husband? Will you love him, comfort him, honour and protect him, and forsaking all others, be faithful to him as long as you both – shall live?

MARGARET. I will.

FATHER. Now, there's another question in this *new* service – to which the answer is 'We will', and that's for all of us to say together. So will you, the family and friends of Margaret and Geoff – support and uphold them in their marriage, now and in . . . and in the years to come?

CONGREGATION. We will.

GEOFF (*whispering*). Which one . . . Which is yours?

FATHER. Repeat after me: Geoffrey, I give you this ring . . .

MARGARET. Geoffrey, I give you this ring . . .

FATHER. . . . as a sign of our marriage . . .

MARGARET. . . . as a sign of our marriage . . .

FATHER. . . . with my body I honour you . . .

MARGARET. . . . with my body I honour you . . .

FATHER. . . . all that I am, I give to you . . .

MARGARET. . . . all that I am, I give to you . . .

FATHER. . . . and all that I have, I share with you . . .

MARGARET. . . . and all that I have, I share with you . . .

FATHER. . . . within the love of God . . .

MARGARET. . . . within the love of God . . .

FATHER. . . . Father, Son, and Holy Spirit . . .

MARGARET. . . . Father, Son and Holy Spirit . . .

A baby in the congregation is babbling and cooing.

GEOFF. . . . Push it on, that's going.

MARGARET *and* GEOFF *laugh softly.*

MARGARET. I'm very hot at the moment.

MARGARET *and* GEOFF *laugh softly.*

GEOFF. That's on. / That's fine.

FATHER. / Well done.

So in the presence of God, and before the *whole* congregation, Margaret and Geoff have given their consent – and made their marriage vows to each other. They have declared their marriage by the joining of hands, and by the giving and receiving of rings. I therefore proclaim that they are husband and wife. Those whom God has joined together – that no one could asunder.

42.

Men Are Pigs (0'54")

Outside the church. MAUREEN *spots her friend* JOY.

MAUREEN. Hi Joy.

JOY. Oh. Hello.

MAUREEN (*laughing*). Hiya.

JOY. We got to see each other in the end. What about it – as well? / What about it?

MAUREEN. / I know, well, of course the last time we were together it was – Jim, wasn't it? (*Laughs.*)

JOY. Oh no. I agree with you. When she rung me up . . .

MAUREEN. I know.

JOY. . . . gobsmacked.

MAUREEN. You know, it was awful what he did to her on the cruise.

JOY. Which one you on about?

MAUREEN. Jim.

JOY. Oh, I know.

MAUREEN. He told her he'd found a / younger woman.

JOY. / Dreadful. I know. Aren't they . . . aren't they pigs, though? They can be pigs, can't they, men?

MAUREEN. Oh, yes. / Yeah, yeah.

JOY. / They can.

MAUREEN. Yes. Jack's supposed to be here as well, Jack the little dancing partner – is he not here?

JOY. Oh yes, he's here. / I met him as well. He's out, he's out. (*Laughs.*)

MAUREEN. / Oh, I haven't seen him. Yeah. Well, she can pass him on to you now.

JOY. Oh. God forbid, God forbid.

MAUREEN *and* JOY *are laughing.*

He can look but not touch.

More laughter.

43.

Somebody Around the Corner (0'54")

Outside the church.

MAUREEN. Hi, you look gorgeous.

MARGARET. Thank you.

MAUREEN *laughs.*

MAUREEN. We're trying to get a picture.

DEREK. We're trying to take a photograph. Don't keep running away.

MAUREEN *laughs.*

MAUREEN. We're trying to take pictures but you didn't stand still long enough.

MARGARET. He says to walk round. (*Referring to* GEOFF.)

MAUREEN. Stand with Geoff a minute.

DEREK (*taking a photo*). That's better. Ahh, now we can see you.

MAUREEN. That's it, we got it. Yeah, I've just met somebody around the corner. / He's a widower, he's a widower and lives rou – An I often see him in the garden and urm, when I went round past his house we started chatting and he's coming to dinner. Well, he invited me to coffee first / but he's coming to dinner. Yeah / And . . . When I saw him in the garden I thought, 'Oh, he's probably a country yokel,' but actually when I've talked to / him, he's well educated and nicely spoken and so on. / (*Laughs.*) Oh look, there's more poses.

PAT. / Have you had the coffee yet with him? Oh, I ooo.

PAT. / Oh, very good. (*Laughs politely.*)

DEREK. / Number forty-five.

PAT. At least. I think more like sixty-five.

DEREK *and* PAT *laugh.*

PAT. / He's not.

PAT. / Oh nice. Good.

44.

Group Photo (0'33")

Outside the church.

PHOTOGRAPHER. Can we have the guests for a group photo, please?

PAT (*to* GEOFF). Oooh, well done.

MARGARET. Group photograph. Group photograph. (*Pause.*) Can you see everyone? / Can everyone see you?

A YOUNG MUM. / Just put her over there for a second.

GEOFF. He can see me, that's all that matters.

PHOTOGRAPHER. Lady with the black coat, now you need to be . . . right . . . This lady in pink is on my end, okay? So anybody . . . Get that side, please.

MARGARET. He's done this before.

GEOFF. I got the sun / in my eyes.

A YOUNG MUM. / Wave at . . . wave at the man.

PHOTOGRAPHER. I can't / see you.

GEOFF. / Look up. (*To* MARGARET.)

ALL. Hooray!

MARGARET *laughs.*

MALE GUEST 1. Hip hip –

ALL. Hooray!

MALE GUEST 1. Hip hip –

ALL. Hooray!

GEOFF. Didn't flash.

General laughter.

A YOUNG MUM. Did you get in the picture?

A YOUNG DAD. No.

A YOUNG MUM. Ooh.

GEOFF. Right, shall we go back and have some fun?

45.

Elite (0'09")

Walking from the church to the reception, passing acquaintances in the street.

MAUREEN. Hello, hello. This is . . . this is only . . . this is only for the elite, so I'm sorry you can't actually come. (*Laughs.*)

46.

Bridesmaids (0'20")

At the reception.

VIVIAN. Erm, I'm Vivian – who's . . . Uncle Geoff's niece, I'm his niece. And this is my husband – David. 'S my sister – (*Laughs.*) Linda. This is her husband, Philip. I said – we were bridesmaids at the first wedding. Won't tell you how many years ago that was. (*Laughs.*)

47a – *simultaneous with 47b*

Brad Pitt (0'37")

At the reception.

JACK. / Did you have anything to do with Margaret's dress? Absolutely wonderful, wasn't it? I saw it close up, as well, it . . . I mean, it looks even better when you get close up. See that – (*Pointing to his place name.*) I'm not . . . well normally. I mean, that's – what they call me, but normally I . . . I'm known as Brad Pitt. (*Laughs.*)

Well, I don't know if they told you the story how I met – Margaret. It wasn't quite so dramatic as Geoff's – meeting. But it was on a cruise. If you go on a cruise, it . . . it . . . The first day, you're sort of – it's a bit – humpty-dumpty, you know. And I went into th . . . the theatre, and there was dancing. I'm very – keen on dancing – there was dancing, and Margaret was dancing with some of the –

47b – *simultaneous with 47a*

Naughty Grandpa (0'15")

At the reception.

MAUREEN. / Hello, are you Geoff's granddaughter? I'm Margaret's friend, and when she first went to stay with him for the weekend, she asked me to go and chaperone her – she asked me to go and chaperone – in case he was a naughty grandpa. (*Laughs.*)

48a – *simultaneous with 48b*

No Romance (1'11")

JACK (*continuing straight on from 47a*). / what they call cruise, um – what do they call them? Uh – the fellas that are employed to – take ladies dancing – well, a 'dancer'. So – the next day, I didn't dance with her, so the next day, she happened to be sitting next to me. And I said, 'Oh, you come from Leominster, do you?' and she said, 'No, it's called "Lemster".' (*Laughing.*) That was the first – clanger I dropped. And then I danced with her – for that cruise I was practically dancing with her every day, you know. And that's how we got to know each other. If I say . . . there's no romance or anything, believe me – you know, 's quite – no relationship whatsoever. Well, she just said . . . she just sorta said, uh, kisses me on the cheek, you know. (*Makes a kissy noise and laughs.*) And when I see Margaret, we'll usually have a dance – I don't know if we'll have one tonight – probably. D . . . do you dance? Oh, p'raps tonight, if you're here. (*Pause.*)We can have a dance. (*Pause.*) I'd be delighted. You see, I'm a widower, of course, / it's my main social activity.

WAITRESS. / White wine, everybody?

JACK. What have you got, dear?

WAITRESS. We got – it's all mixture, it's all for sort . . . we didn't get the wine.

JACK. I don . . . I don't mind. / Whichever you like.

WAITRESS. / It's wet.

JACK. I say . . . I said to Margaret last night, I said, 'Are we going to do the rumba?' because she does a wonderful rumba, Margaret.

48b – *simultaneous with 48a*

Taller (0'23")

At the reception.

MAUREEN. / I'm Maureen, Margaret's friend. And I chaperoned Margaret the first time she went for the weekend with Geoff. Aren't you like your father? (*Laughs.*) Except you're taller. Yeah. (*Laughs.*) Are you going back to America afterwards? See, my son-in-law's American. From, um, Los Angeles. We had the wedding in Surrey, but then we had a big do in Los Angeles for all the Americans. Yeah, so that's nice.

49.

A Weird Dream (3'09")

At the reception.

GEOFF *bangs loudly on the table.*

MARGARET. Let me have a drink before you speak.

GEOFF. All right. Now comes the time with trepidation.

The guests join GEOFF *and* MARGARET *in laughter.*

Well, first of all – I'd like to thank Margaret for – giving up all her spare time, and – consenting to marry me today.

General laughter.

I'm sure . . . I'm sure we'll be happy together. We have a lot in common, and uh – I'm sure that will be go . . . that will go a long way. I'd like to thank you all for coming. And I've got – someone right at the far end there I'd want to thank. I'd like to thank *Maureen* for – smoothing over our – first path. When uh – we met on the cruise, um, I – you know, I thought I was doing so well, I said . . . I said to Margaret, 'Would you like to come and stay at my place for the weekend?', and she – said, 'Well, I don't know you well enough to come and stay at your place for the weekend.' So I says, 'Well, what do you need?' So she says, 'Well, I'll come if I can bring a friend.' Well, Maureen came as the friend, and I think she was complaining about – playing *gooseberry* all the weekend or something or other . . .

General laughter.

Now, have I met . . . left anybody out with regards to – thanking people? Cos . . . my . . . when you get to my age, your memory gets a bit short, sort of thing.

General laughter.

I . . . I . . . I can remember things fifty years ago, but things that happened yesterday – sort of slip my mind. Which sort of . . . well, it . . . it rather – reminds me of a – uh, a joke that a friend told me – a little while ago, about this elderly gentleman th . . . that met a lady on a cruise, who was a few years younger – than himself. And he took a fancy to her, and uh – he courted her for a number of months, and they got on very well together. After about – ten months or so of – courting her, he decided to – ask her to marry him. She had a little think, she said, 'Oh yes, yes I will.' Well, anyway – that particular night – he had a . . . a weird dream, and he woke up, and he thought – to himself, 'Did she say yes or no?' And this worried him, and he couldn't get to sleep again. So he thought, 'Well, the only thing I can do', following morning, 'is to phone her up.' So he phoned her up, and he said, 'Do you remember last night?' So she says 'Yes.' So he says – 'Do you remember I asked you to marry me?' So she says, '*Oh, yes!*' And he said, 'What did you say?' She says – 'Oh, I said yes.' And he said, 'Well, you know I . . . uh – I'm so ashamed of meself, you know, forgetting – whether you said yes or no.' So she says, 'Oh, you don't want to worry about things like that,' she says – 'I've got a short memory too.' She says, 'I had this terrible dream in the night, and I woke up,' and she thought – 'Oh, I said yes to someone –

The guests begin to laugh.

– but I can't remember which one it was.'

Clapping and general laughter.

Well, anyway, I – I think . . . I've said enough . . .

MARGARET. You have. (*Chuckles.*)

GEOFF (*laughs*). Uh – the story was a bit too near the home. (*Laughs.*) Anyway, thank you very much for coming.

Clapping.

50.

Band of Gold (0'25")

At the reception.

MARGARET. Could you go and put on the . . . the the ther's
urm . . . on the one that says 'Band of Gold', there's . . .
I think it's number four. It's 'I Just Called to Say I Love
You' – that's our tune. (*To* GEOFF.) I'm going to dance
with you.

GEOFF. Eh?

MARGARET. I haven't danced with you all night.

GEOFF. Shall we go down here? We'll go down here. Come
on, bring your wine. Eh? Bring your wine. We'll go down
here.

51a – *simultaneous with 51b*

The Cha Cha Cha (2'38")

At the reception. GEOFF *and* MARGARET *dance to 'I Just
Called to Say I Love You'.*

51b – *simultaneous with 51a*

Bail Out (0'02")

At the reception. Shortly after GEOFF *and* MARGARET *start
dancing,* JACK *gets up and exits.*

JACK. I think I'm going to bail out, I'll be back shortly.

> JACK *re-enters during the song, dancing with another
> guest, up-staging* MARGARET *and* GEOFF. *He is now
> dressed in a blazer and tie, with dance shoes.*

52.

Are You Going to Feel Lonely? (0'35")

At the end of the reception.

MAUREEN. Are you – going to feel lonely?

JACK. Well, it's packed up so early. I was a bit disappointed really, cos I was looking forward to – having a sort of dance with, uh Margaret. Margaret was a . . . was a bit disappointed cos she said to me, 'Oh well, we didn't get that dance after all, did we?' I've got my dance shoes on, look, yeah. See, I thought we were going to have a dance.

MAUREEN. So, are you going home tomorrow?

JACK. Yeah, that's right, after breakfast.

MAUREEN. 'Spect you feel a bit sad.

JACK. Well, no – um. I . . . I . . . I'm sure things'll – turn out fine. (*Pause.*) She's a good-hearted lady, isn't she?

MAUREEN. Oh yeah.

JACK. That's one of her characteristics, Margaret.

MAUREEN. Yes, she's very caring.

JACK. Oh very. / Very. Very caring.

MAUREEN. / Mmm.

53.

Frizzy Hair & An Animal is Company (2'02")

MAUREEN's living room. She strokes a cat on her lap.

MAUREEN. I think he – he would have liked to be in Geoff's position, but he's accepted that he's not. I mean, he's not nearly as well off as Geoff. Yeah, an . . . Margaret's hair looked much nicer than it normally . . . I think she must have had the girl go to her house and do it. Normally

Margaret has her hair rather frizzy and old fashioned. But it was nice and *smooth*.

My days of travelling so much are – coming to an end. And – an animal is company. And he's um – oh, he's very loving and he follows me everywhere and he's always on my lap, you know. He's company and I can talk to him – but I don't let him in my bedroom at nights, cos he – one day his position might be usurped – (*Laughing.*) and then he'll take a dim view of it. (*Laughs.*)

What I want to do is take it slowly like, you see, Margaret took it slowly with him because she wasn't all that keen. You see, when I've really liked somebody, I've . . . because at my age you don't have to worry – about getting pregnant or anything. But a man may seem perfectly normal and nice, but he could still be . . . have something that he could give you. (*Coughs.*) I mean, the three men that I've been with – yeah, on the surface they've all seemed very nice respectable men, but then – if you sl . . . just sleep with that one, you may have slept with twenty in a way – cos they've slept with somebody else, they've slept with somebody else and so on, you know. And I thought, you know, I thought about this German – I thought, 'He's so attractive', you know, 'I do want to go to bed with him' – but it's a bit difficult for me to say to him, (*Laughing.*) 'Where's your certificate?' I don't know quite what to do about that, you see. But, I mean, he's probably a greater risk than a lot – here – you know, living in Germany. I don't know. (*Pause.*) And then of course, I did sleep with um – Bernard. (*Laughs.*) But it wasn't very good. That's what put me off, really. I mean, I . . . I thought it was inevitable – when he came up.

54.

The Spark Didn't Ignite (0'36")

BERNARD*'s study.*

BERNARD. I went down there full of hope and expectation and the *spark didn't ignite*. Part of the trouble, sweetie, is that *I'm* an silly old *romantic*. I'm not really into sex without *love*. (*Laughs gently.*) And so, you know, err I mean – we – we – we – we *slept* together urm but it wasn't *much*. But that was the trouble because I had recognised that I wasn't going to fall in love with her.

55.

The World's Best Lover (0'57")

MAUREEN*'s living room.*

MAUREEN. He wasn't a very good lover. And he hurt me. And, um, I said it hurt me and he said, oh, that put him off, he said, if he thinks it's hurting a woman. But . . . he's got a good body for his age. But – I mean, David was the world's best lover really, and that's why nobody since has – pleased me. That's why I still think about him. But he won't talk to me. So – yes, it's sad he won't talk to me. But, to be honest, after meeting forty-four I was beginning to think whether I'll ever be really keen on anybody again.

Pause.

Haven't you got beautiful whiskers, darling? You've got lovely whiskers, yes you have, you've got beautiful whiskers. They are *very* beautiful. Yes.

She sighs.

Ooh.

The End.

(Total Running Time: 1'11'26")

Simon Burt
BOTTLE UNIVERSE
GOT TO BE HAPPY

Caryl Churchill
BLUE HEART
CHURCHILL PLAYS: THREE
CHURCHILL: SHORTS
CLOUD NINE
A DREAM PLAY *after* Strindberg
FAR AWAY
HOTEL
ICECREAM
LIGHT SHINING IN BUCKINGHAMSHIRE
MAD FOREST
A NUMBER
THE SKRIKER
THIS IS A CHAIR
THYESTES *after* Seneca
TRAPS

Ariel Dorfman
DEATH AND THE MAIDEN
READER
THE RESISTANCE TRILOGY
WIDOWS

Emma Frost
AIRSICK

Debbie Tucker Green
BORN BAD
DIRTY BUTTERFLY
STONING MARY
TRADE & GENERATIONS

Ayub Khan-Din
EAST IS EAST
LAST DANCE AT DUM DUM
NOTES ON FALLING LEAVES

Tony Kushner
ANGELS IN AMERICA – PARTS ONE & TWO
HOMEBODY/KABUL

A Nick Hern Book

Cruising first published in Great Britain as a paperback original
in 2006 by Nick Hern Books Limited, 14 Larden Road,
London W3 7ST in association with The Bush Theatre, London

Cruising copyright © 2006 Alecky Blythe

Alecky Blythe has asserted her right to be identified as
the author of this work

Cover image: 'Dancing on the QE2' from *The Bumper Edition* by
Beryl Cook © 2000 Beryl Cook. Permission granted c/o Rogers,
Coleridge & White Ltd

Typeset by Country Setting, Kingsdown, Kent CT14 8ES
Printed and bound in Great Britain by Biddles, King's Lynn

A CIP catalogue record for this book is available from
the British Library

ISBN-13   978 1 85459 937 7
ISBN-10   1 85459 937 2